To make words sing
Is a wonderful thing—
Because in a song
Words last so long.

—Langston Hughes

poems by
LANGSTON HUGHES

sail away

art by
ASHLEY BRYAN

atheneum

Atheneum Books for Young Readers
New York London Toronto Sydney New Delhi

Illustrator's Note

The scissors shown on the endpapers are the scissors that my mother used in sewing and embroidery and that I, in turn, used in cutting the colored papers for all the collage compositions in this book.

atheneum

ATHENEUM BOOKS FOR YOUNG READERS
An imprint of Simon & Schuster Children's Publishing Division
1230 Avenue of the Americas, New York, New York 10020
Text copyright 1921–1958 by Langston Hughes, copyright renewed. Reprinted from:
The Collected Poems of Langston Hughes. Copyright © 1994 by The Estate of Langston Hughes.
Published by arrangement with Alfred A. Knopf, an imprint of The Knopf Doubleday
Publishing Group, a division of Penguin Random House LLC
Illustrations copyright © 2015 by Ashley Bryan

For information about special discounts for bulk purchases, please contact
Simon & Schuster Special Sales at 1-866-506-1949 or business@simonandschuster.com.
The Simon & Schuster Speakers Bureau can bring authors to your live event. For more
information or to book an event, contact the Simon & Schuster Speakers Bureau
at 1-866-248-3049 or visit our website at www.simonspeakers.com.
Book design by Ann Bobco
The text for this book is set in DK Crayon Crumble, Neutraface Text, and Gill Sans Standard.
The illustrations for this book are rendered with paper collages.
Manufactured in China
0615 SCP
First Edition
10 9 8 7 6 5 4 3 2 1
Library of Congress Cataloging-in-Publication Data
Hughes, Langston, 1902–1967.
[Poems. Selections]
Sail away / Langston Hughes ; illustrated by Ashley Bryan. — First edition.
pages cm
ISBN 978-1-4814-3085-2
I. Sea poetry, American. I. Bryan, Ashley, illustrator. II. Title.
PS3515.U274A6 2015
811'.52—dc23   2014035769

To the memory of
poet Langston Hughes,
who made words sing,
and
to my friend
poet Nikki Giovanni,
who makes words sing
—A. B.

Catch

Big Boy came
Carrying a mermaid
On his shoulders
And the mermaid
Had her tail
Curved
Beneath his arm.

Being a fisher boy,
He'd found a fish
To carry—
Half fish,
Half girl
To marry.

Long Trip

The sea is a wilderness of waves,
A desert of water.
We dip and dive,
Rise and roll,
Hide and are hidden
On the sea.
    Day, night,
    Night, day,
The sea is a desert of waves,
A wilderness of water.

Water-Front Streets

The spring is not so beautiful there—
 But dream ships sail away
To where the spring is wondrous rare
 And life is gay.

The spring is not so beautiful there—
 But lads put out to sea
Who carry beauties in their hearts
 And dreams, like me.

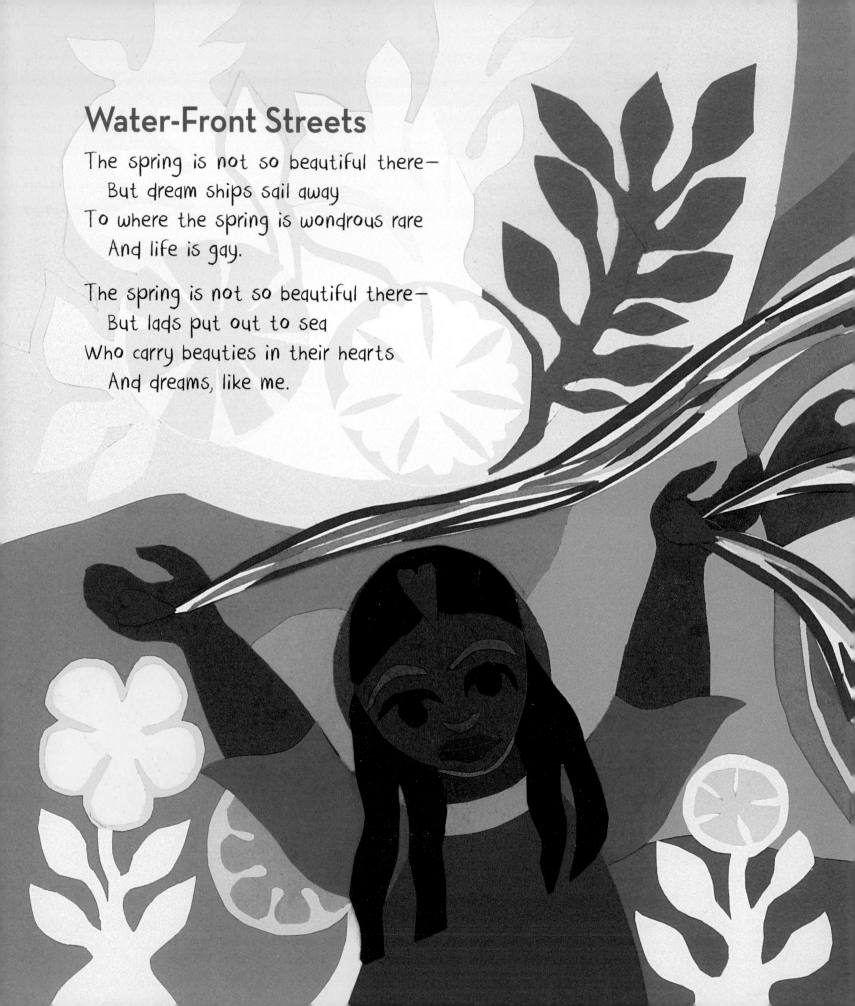

Seascape

Off the coast of Ireland
As our ship passed by
We saw a line of fishing ships
Etched against the sky.

Off the coast of England
As we rode the foam
We saw an Indian merchantman
Coming home.

Moonlight Night: Carmel

Tonight the waves march
In long ranks
Cutting the darkness
With their silver shanks,
Cutting the darkness
And kissing the moon
And beating the land's
Edge into a swoon.

Sailor

He sat upon the rolling deck
Half a world away from home,
And smoked a Capstan cigarette
And watched the blue waves tipped with foam.

He had a mermaid on his arm,
An anchor on his breast,
And tattooed on his back he had
A blue bird in a nest.

Sea Calm

How still,
How strangely still
The water is today.
It is not good
For water
To be so still that way.

Fulfillment

The earth-meaning
Like the sky-meaning
Was fulfilled.

We got up
And went to the river,
Touched silver water,
Laughed and bathed
In the sunshine.

Day
Became a bright ball of light
For us to play with,
Sunset
A yellow curtain,
Night
A velvet screen.

Sea Charm

Sea charm
The sea's own children
Do not understand.
They know
But that the sea is strong
Like God's hand.
They know
But that sea wind is sweet
Like God's breath,
And that the sea holds
A wide, deep death.

April Rain Song

Let the rain kiss you.
Let the rain beat upon your
    head with silver liquid drops.
Let the rain sing you a lullaby.

The rain makes still pools on the
    sidewalk.
The rain makes running pools in the gutter,
The rain plays a little sleep song
    on our roof at night—

And I love the rain.

F

There was a fish
With a greedy eye
Who darted toward
A big green fly.

Alas! That fly
Was bait on a hook!
So the fisherman took
The fish home to cook.

Jaime

He sits on a hill
And beats a drum
For the great earth spirits
That never come.

He sits on a hill
Looking out to sea
Toward a mirage-land
That will never be.

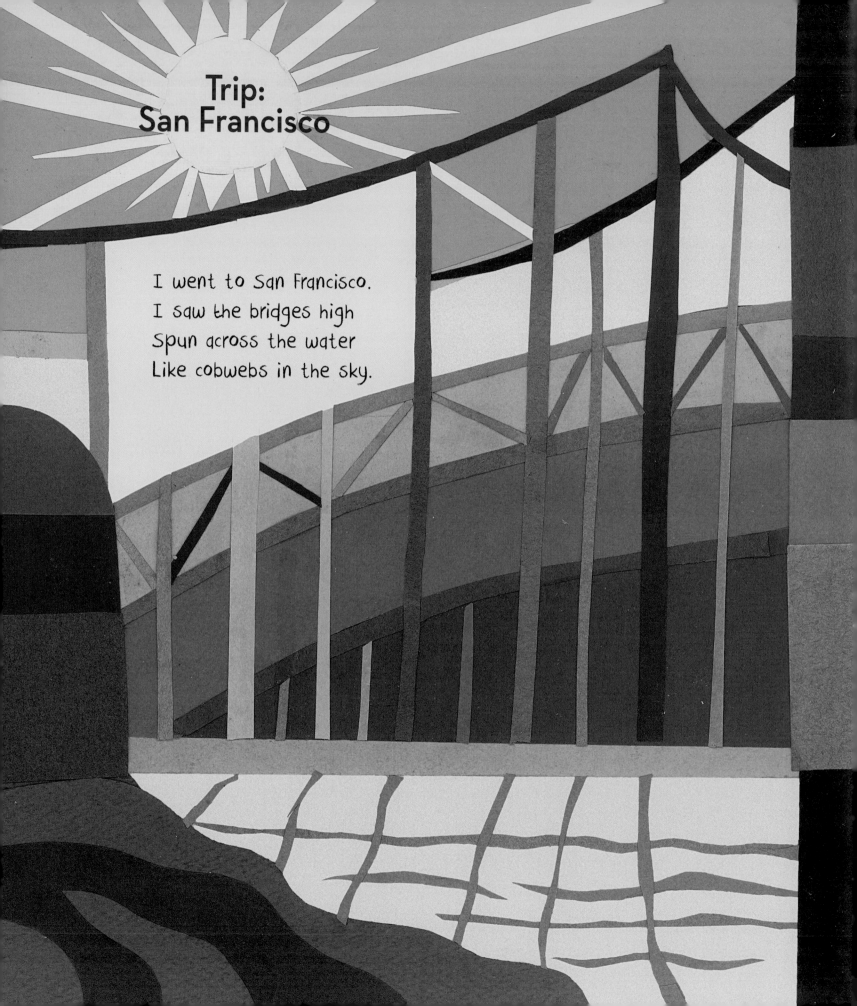

Trip: San Francisco

I went to San Francisco.
I saw the bridges high
Spun across the water
Like cobwebs in the sky.

My Loves

I love to see the big white moon,
  A-shining in the sky,
I love to see the little stars,
  When the shadow clouds go by.

I love the rain drops falling
  On my roof-top in the night;
I love the soft wind's sighing,
  Before the dawn's gray light.

I love the deepness of the blue,
  In my Lord's heaven above;
But better than all these things
      I think,
I love my lady love.

The Negro Speaks of Rivers

I've known rivers:
I've known rivers ancient as the world and older than the
    flow of human blood in human veins.

My soul has grown deep like the rivers.

I bathed in the Euphrates when dawns were young.
I built my hut near the Congo and it lulled me to sleep.
I looked upon the Nile and raised the pyramids above it.
I heard the singing of the Mississippi when Abe Lincoln
    went down to New Orleans, and I've seen its muddy
    bosom turn all golden in the sunset.

I've known rivers:
Ancient, dusky rivers.

My soul has grown deep like the rivers.